Freight Train
Donald Crews

PHOENIX YARD BOOKS

Freight Train
ISBN: 978-1-907912-10-8

First published by Greenwillow Books,
New York, 1978

This edition published in Great Britain
by Phoenix Yard Books Ltd, 2012

Phoenix Yard Books
Phoenix Yard
65 King's Cross Road
London WC1X 9LW
www.phoenixyardbooks.com

Published by arrangement with HarperCollins
Children's Books, a division of HarperCollins
Publishers, New York

1 3 5 7 9 10 8 6 4 2

A CIP catalogue record for this book is
available from the British Library

Phoenix Yard design by A+B Studio
Printed in China

With due respect to Casey Jones, John Henry, The Rock Island Line,
and the countless freight trains passed and passing the big house in Cottondale

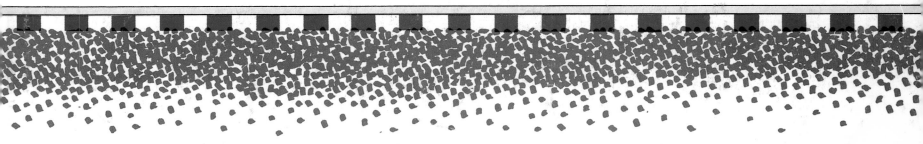

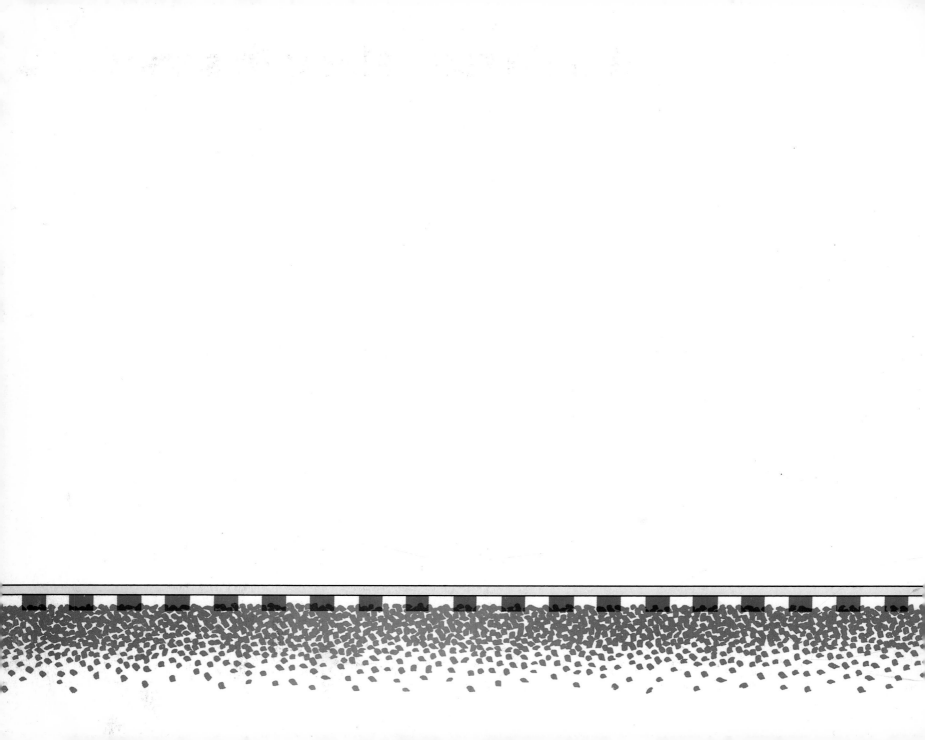

A train runs along this track.

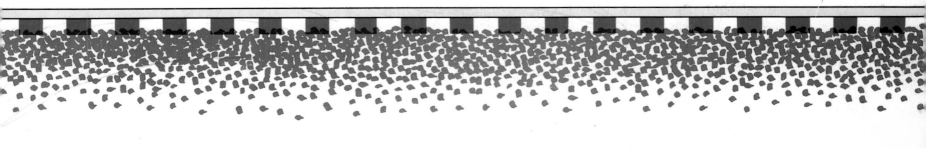

Red guard's van at the back

Orange petrol tanker next

Yellow grain
hopper

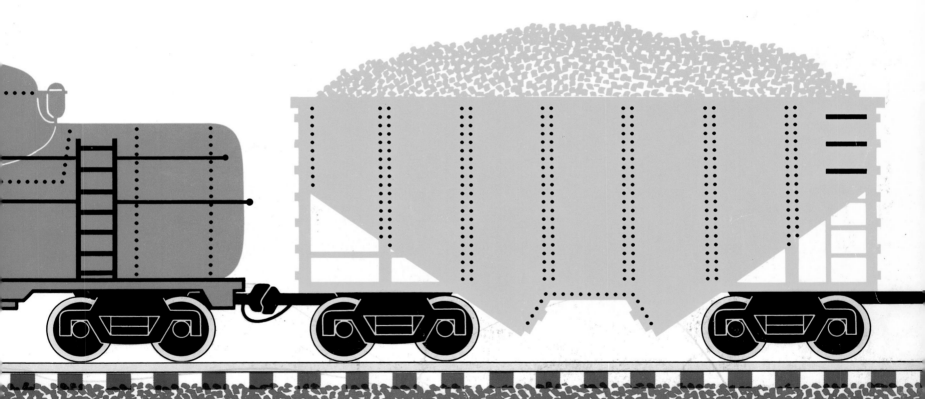

**Green
cattle truck**

**Blue
coal
truck**

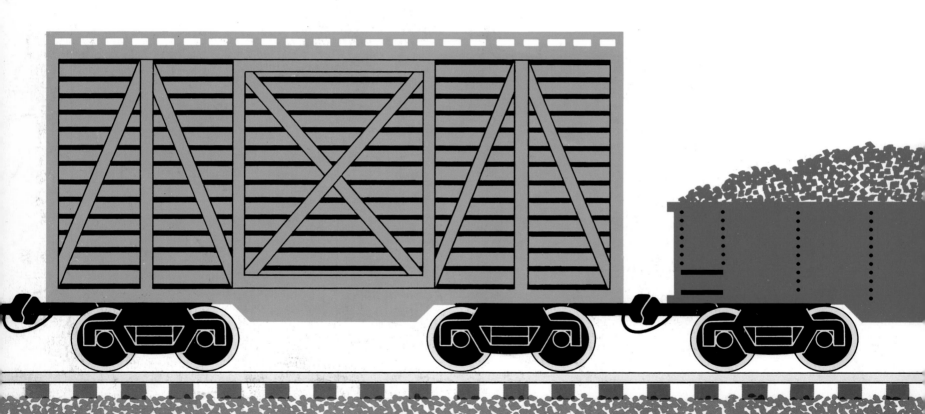

Purple
fruit van

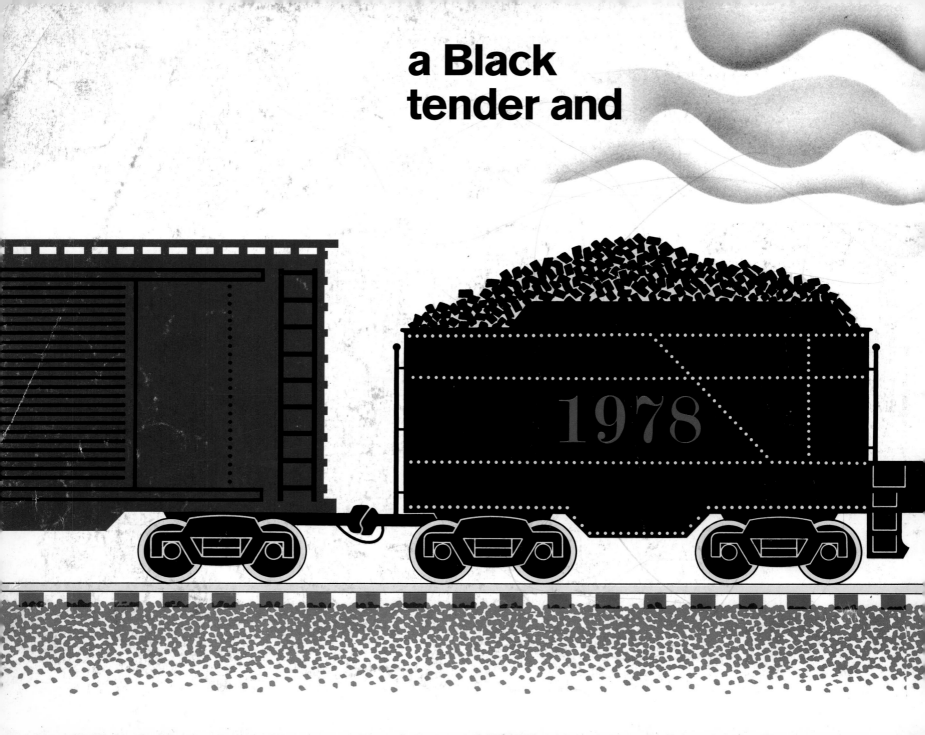

a Black
tender and

Freight train.

Moving.

Going through tunnels

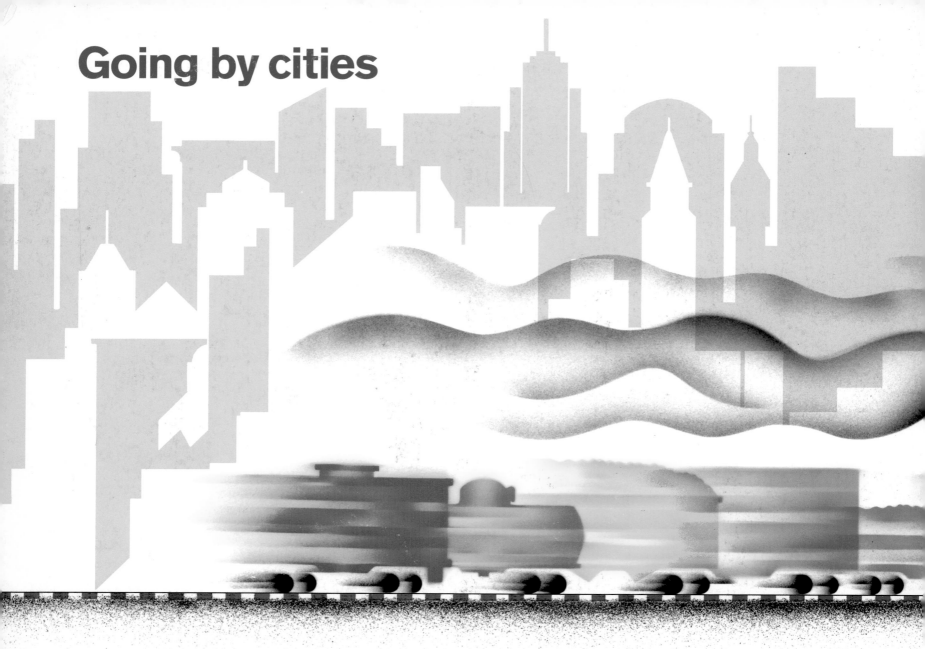

Crossing bridges.

Moving in darkness.